Faith
&
Doubt

Faith
&
Doubt

Poems for Troubled Times

Jane Starwood

These poems are dedicated
to the suffering world.
May they help rekindle the
faith of all those who ponder
them with open hearts.

These Words

These words are weak vessels
They cannot hold the fulness of my heart

They spill and crack
They overflow and flood
The plains of my prayers

O Father, strengthen my words
To match my love for Thee!

Thicken their sinews
Embolden their blood
And the marrow of their bones

Let me write Thee in my heart
And the hearts of Thy people!

Let my words partake of Thy power
Let them live!
Let them move
And have their being in Thee

Father, I am Thine
Let my words also be Thine!

God is in the Storm

God is in the storm
And in the calm

He's in the lamentation
And the psalm

He meets me in the desert
And on the raging sea

He finds me in my sorrow
Wherever I may be

He gives me living water
To soothe my thirsting soul

And when my heart is shattered
Only He can make me whole

His Path

He bids us to become
as little children,
meek and lowly,
with joyful hearts,
and soft steps,
walking in His path.

His yoke is as easy
as a garland of flowers,
His burden as light
as a crown of feathers.
Thus arrayed,
we will follow Him,
dancing in His path.

Not My Own

I thought I was my own
I thought all hope was vain
For any loving God
To save the world from pain

I sought for earthly things
For pleasures large and small
To fill the empty hours
'Til death had claimed them all

But I was not my own
For Christ redeemed my soul
He paid for all my sins
His suffering made me whole

With broken heart I knelt
And wept for all my wrongs
His virtue washed me clean
Then joy became my song

Now when I kneel and pray
"Father, make me thine,"
I hear these precious words:
"Daughter, you are Mine!"

O Father

O Father
Will You fill my cup
With good things from above
With peace and joy
And charity
With hope and lasting love

O Father
Will you teach my heart
All of Thy Son's ways
And help me walk
Along His path
As I live out my days

Man of Sorrow

Why did He come
This perfect Man
This God from on high?

Why did He come
To drown in our sorrows
And partake of our grief?

Why did He come
To wade through our guilt
And sink in our sins?

Why did He come
To suffer the pain
Of the blind
The lame
The leprous?

He came because
With His Father
He made us
And He loves us
As a Father loves
His sickly child
His wayward son
His rebellious daughter

He came to rescue us
The faithful
And the undeserving

He reached down to us
That we might
Reach up to Him

He suffered with us
That we might
Have joy with Him

He died for us
That we might
Live with Him

Forever

Never Let Me Stray

When I can feel
My pride rise up
Please help me knock it down

When doubts assail
My troubled mind
Please keep my soul unbound

For I would serve
My wounded Lord
Who died to set me free

Who drank the cup
Of bitterness
And bled on Calvary

Give me a meek
And lowly heart
On bended knees I pray

Let pride and doubt
Depart from me
Lord, never let me stray

One Aim

Let charity and mercy
Fill me to the brim
Let all my life
Have this one aim:
Emulating Him

New Psalm One

Day and night, in all things,
I wait on the goodness and mercy of my Lord,
Who knows my every need
And supplies it with abundance,
Who knows every prayer of my heart
And answers with His bounteous grace,
Who sees my tears and sheds His own,
Who hears my laughter and smiles.
I will praise God's name forever.

One Taste

Through the mist she made her way
Fast holding to the rod
Step by step she hurried on
Toward the things of God

When at length she gained her goal
She stood beneath the Tree
And reaching up, she plucked the Fruit
Whose flesh would make her free

In whiteness it surpassed the snow
Its fragrance pure and sweet
She marveled at the wondrous gift
And then began to eat

Just one bite had passed her lips
Just one small, precious taste
When she heard the multitude
And turned to look in haste

From across a dark divide
Arose the jeering sound
As she heeded all their scorn
The Fruit dropped to the ground

Filled with shame, she walked away
And left the Fruit behind
Its fulness she would never know
For pride had made her blind

Leap of Faith

It is not easy to follow Him
The path He walks is long and rough
Dust blinds our eyes
Stones trip our feet

We may lose sight of Him
And wander down strange roads
Before we find His footprints
In the desert sand

We may come to the edge of a cliff
And see Him far below
Beckoning to us
But we cannot see a way down

That is when we must gather our courage
Gird up our strength
And take a leap of faith
Into His open arms

My All

Where I am weak
He makes me strong

When I would faint
He bears me up

In the midst of grief
He dries my tears

In the throes of pain
He heals my wounds

He is my All
My Everything

My life, my joy
I owe to Him
Who ransomed me
From death and sin

Roll the Stone Away

Roll the stone away
It is not heavy
For He makes our
Burdens light

Roll the stone away
From the empty tomb
For He is not dead
But rose for us
That we may rise

Roll the stone away
And free your heart
From pain and fear

Roll the stone away
And forgive all the
Wrongs of the past

Roll the stone away
And live forever
In His love

The Foolish Sailor

In a small boat
I drifted from shore
Onto a storm-tossed sea

No rudder
No oars
No sail
No instruments
To read the skies
Or plumb the depths

I even left behind
The Master
Who could have calmed
The wind
And the waves
And steered me
Safely home

I didn't know
He followed me
Walking on the water
Waiting for me to turn
And reach for Him

He Came as a Babe

He came as a babe
And grew to a man
Though not just a man
But a God

He humbled Himself
To teach us the way
To walk in the path
That He trod

He offered Himself
A ransom for sin
He suffered, He bled
And He died

Then rose from the grave
That we might arise
In eternal light
To abide

His Grace

Let His grace
Heal your heart
Soothe your soul
And ease your sorrow

Let His Son
Share your grief
Mourn with you
And lift you up

Let His mercy
Cover your sins
Wash you clean
And give you joy
Everlasting

In the Darkness of Gethsemane

In the darkness of Gethsemane
The Savior knelt to pray,
"Father, if it be Thy will,
Please take this cup away."

Yet He knew His mortal life
Was coming to an end.
He'd done all things required of Him,
And now He must descend.

His Parents wept to see the blood
Upon that noble brow,
The Great Jehovah on His knees
Fulfilling every vow.

The pain began, the suffering
For every human sin.
The torment of each mortal soul
Filled Him to the brim.

Willingly He took the weight
Upon his tortured frame.
Willingly He offered up
Himself to take the blame.

His back was bent,
His head was bowed,
He drank deep from the well.
Our sins rose up and dragged Him through
The very gates of hell.

As dawn rose on Gethsemane,
Christ struggled to his feet.
The cross still lay ahead of Him
Who owns the Judgment Seat.

As angels watched in silent awe,
He staggered with his cross.
None other could have paid the price
To ransom all the lost.

And as He hung in agony,
His mother looking on,
With failing breath He said the words,
"Father, it is done."

Let not his sacrifice be vain!
Come walk the path He trod!
From Heaven through Gethsemane,
He leads us Home to God.

How Sweet the Words

How sweet the words
My soul does hear
When I kneel to pray

How sweet the love
You proffer me
Every night and day

How sweet the song
That fills my heart
With Your joy divine

How sweet to know
That at long last
I am truly Thine

New Psalm Twenty-Three

The Lord of love is my guide.
I need no other.
His loving-kindness brings me peaceful rest.
He calms the raging waters of my soul.
Along paths of light and wisdom,
I follow in my Lord's footsteps.
Though harm and even death may threaten,
In God's presence I am not afraid.
God's laws are my truth,
And God's words my lifeline.
Doubt and distrust may assail me on all sides,
But I am safe at my Lord's table,
Where I am honored and comforted
Far beyond my worth.
Surely God's astonishing gifts are mine always,
And the door of His kingdom is open to me forever.

What Will You Seek?

Will you seek
The shiny trinkets
Of the fallen world
Or the true riches
Of your Father's throne?

Will you join
The vast multitudes
Of faithless scoffers
Or always hold fast
To the rod of iron?

Will you let
Your testimony
Wither, fade, and die
Or tend and feed it
Every night and day?

23

Will you shun
His Holy Spirit
And let His whispers
Withdraw and vanish
From your rebellious soul?

Will you choose
To harden your heart
Against our dear Christ
Or turn and rush back
Into His waiting arms?

The Sower and the Harvest

Plant the Word
In a ready heart
And rejoice as it grows

Plant the Word
In a stony heart
And sorrow when it dies

Plant the Word
In a doubting heart
And it might lie fallow
For a season
Or a dozen seasons
Before it springs
To everlasting life

Plant the Word
In many hearts
For the sower knows not
His harvest

Wounded Hearts

Of all the hurts the human heart can hold,
The sharpest are the hurts we felt of old,
When those we loved,
Who should have held us dear,
Instead made us to sorrow and to fear.
The scars we bear are thus so deep and broad,
No one can understand except our God.
He sent His Son to bleach the darkest stain,
To take away our sorrow and our pain.
If we accept the price He gladly paid,
The wounds that scar our hearts begin to fade,
And from that moment we can start to live,
If we but find the courage to forgive.

On My Knees

On my knees
I bare my soul
And break my heart for Him

From my knees
He lifts me up
And makes me whole again

Thy Will

Teach me all Thy will
I care not for my own
Let my heart grow soft
Not hardened like a stone

Father, let Thy will
Be written on my heart
Come and dwell in me
And nevermore depart

Face to Face

There is a Book in heaven
Wherein our sins are writ
But we can blot them out
And be pure every whit

Our dear Christ ransomed us
In sorrow and in pain
To wipe those pages clean
And lead us home again

If we endure in faith
And keep our covenants strong
If we on bended knee
Repent from all our wrongs

Then we will enter in
With glory and with grace
To gain celestial crowns
And see God face to face

Doubt

Place your doubts
In a knapsack
And carry them
On your back
As you walk
The covenant path
Toward God

Shed them
One by one
As you grow
In knowledge
And in faith
Enduring at last
To the end

Heavenly Mother

I sense my Mother's presence
Somewhere beyond the veil
I feel Her arms around me
Every time I try and fail

I know my Mother loves me
With all a parent's care
She stands beside my Father
Though I cannot see her there

Someday I'll get to meet Her
And tell Her face to face
How much I came to love Her
As I grew from grace to grace

And we will dwell together
In Their bright home above
With all my earthly loved ones
In joy and heavenly love

His Light

You dwell in a fallen world
On an island set apart
You wear our dear Christ's armor
Against the fiery darts

But if one should penetrate
Where your armor has grown weak
And you are lured away
From that true joy you seek

Or if you should wander down
Darkened roads that lead to sin
You can return to Him
By His good lamp within

His light still burns inside you
Even when you go astray
Let it lead you homeward
And He will guide your way

For this great gift He gave you
When He suffered death and pain
That in Godly sorrow
You might be His again

Back Home

In these last days,
The pull of the world
Grows ever stronger

It would be so easy
To give in and grasp
The pleasures and treasures
Glittering brightly on the horizon
Just within reach

When your eyes are blinded
By the sparkle and shine,
Your ears deafened
By the cacophony of voices,
You cannot see
What you would leave behind

You cannot hear
The still small voice
Calling your name

But sooner or later,
That world you envy
Will swallow you whole,
Devour you
And spit you out,
Spent and longing
For all you've lost

It's not too late to reclaim
The blessings that await you,
If you will only turn
And follow His path
Back Home

Peace

His peace He gives us
Not the world's peace
But the peace of heaven
The peace of following Him
The peace of knowing
We are His
That our trials are temporary
And for our good

Knowing this
We can bear
Even pain
Even loss
Even grief
With His peace
Alive in our hearts

Pride

Pride is my false armor
Against armies of doubt

Pride lifts me up
Above the crowd

Pride hardens my heart
And dims my eyes
Stops my ears
And dulls my faith

Pride steals me away
From truth and light
Into the darkness
Of the world

Lord, deliver me
And keep me safe
From the sin of pride

For Us

His arms of mercy
Stretch wide
To receive all
Who come to Him
On their knees
With broken hearts
And contrite spirits
Trusting in
His sacrifice
For us
His suffering
For us
His death
For us
His triumph
For us
As He descended
And then rose
For us
That we may rise
With Him

Freedom

Do you think you'll be free
Out there in the world
Without divine law
To guide you?

Do you think you'll be free
From sorrow for sin
If you cast Christ's love
Behind you?

Do you think you'll be free
When you leave the fold
Hoping the Shepherd
Won't find you?

Will you still think you're free
When you let your doubts
Entangle your soul
And bind you?

The Chasm

I dug it with a spade of doubt
I dug it deep and wide
Until one day I clambered out
Upon the other side

Looking back, I could not see
All I had left behind
A veil had dropped in front of me
A mist that left me blind

My rebel heart had captured me
And led me far astray
I thought the world had set me free
I thought I knew the way

I wandered far beyond the mark
But every now and then
The Light of Christ threw off a spark
Illuminating Him

His Loving Eyes

When He called His disciples
He knew who they were
He'd known them through eons of time

When He calls His dear prophets
We know that they were
His brothers in precincts divine

When He looks at God's children
Through His loving eyes
He sees the true spirit we hide

And He urges us onward
Through troubles and trials
So we may return to His side

Little Lamb

Little lamb
Do you know
You are lost?
Do you know
The Good Shepherd
Searches for you?

Oh, He knows
Where you are.
His search is for
The way to reach
Your doubting heart.

Little lamb
Do you know
You are lost?

Such a Love

How can we fathom
Such a love?
The firstborn Son of God
Almighty Jehovah
Creator of worlds
Commander of sea and storm
Brought to His knees
By our pain
Our sins
Our sorrows
Bleeding
Broken
Torn
Tormented
In a garden
In a court
On a cross
As He died for us
For us!
How can we so live
To be worthy of
Such a love?

Repentance

Let my sins
Drive me to my knees
In humble prayer
Before my God

Let my tears
Bathe the wounded feet
Of my dear Savior
Day and night

Let my heart
Break upon the rocks
Of my foolish pride
As I pray

Let my soul
Be cleansed in His blood
Who died for my sins
In great love

Let my voice
Rise in praise of Him
Singing songs of joy
In His name

Silence

When you can't hear your Father's voice
Be still and know He's there
Wait in all humility
To feel His tender care

We do not see His purposes
We cannot know His ways
We only know He teaches us
And counts our earthly days

In silence there can be great joy
In silence love shines through
No words can tell the matchless love
Our Father feels for you

So wait and watch in love and faith
In meekness and in peace
For we know not the day and hour
Our mortal trials will cease

You Are There

Lost in my grief
I reach for You
And you are always there

Mired in my sins
I call to You
And You do hear my prayer

Captured by doubt
I turn my back
But You do not depart

And when I turn
To look for You
You calm my troubled heart

Lifted in love
I'll cling to You
Through all my mortal years

Until I step
Through that bright veil
And You dry all my tears

Listen

Close your door
Silence your phone
Quiet your mind
Calm your heart

Pray–

Listen–

With a calm heart
With a quiet mind

Listen–

And you will hear Him

The Tree of Life

Come into the sheltering shade
Of the Tree of Life

Partake of the fruit of the tree
And let go of strife

Drink deep of the gospel of Christ
Let it fill your cup

And dwell in the light of His love
Ever lifted up

Second Coming

On that bright day when Christ returns
Clothed in glory, where will you stand?

Will you be wheat among the tares
Plucked to safety by angelic hands?

Or will you shrink in guilt and fear
Knowing you've lost the promised land?

While chaos reigns will you prepare?
Will you hold fast to that iron rod?

Will you drink deep from His proffered cup
And follow where His feet have trod?

On that bright day where will you stand?
At Satan's side, or with our God?

That Bright Day

Keep your lamp of faith filled
And your oil of diligence replenished
For the time is short
Until Christ returns in glory

Do not wait until
The wick burns low
Or the oil is on sale
At half price

The time to prepare is now
For only the Father knows
The hour of His Son's coming

Watch and wait
Not in fear
But in glad anticipation
For those whose lamps
Burn true
Will rise up rejoicing
On that bright day

The Eyes of the Prophets

The eyes of the prophets
Pierce us to our souls

The words of the prophets
Teach God's will for us

The hearts of the prophets
Break for all our pain

The love of the prophets
Lifts us up to Christ
And sends us home again

Through His Eyes

Look through His eyes
At a suffering soul
What do you see?
A tender heart
Filled with pain
Armed with angry words
Or armored silence

What would He do
But open wide His arms
In silent love
Or speak soft words
Filled with peace
And balm for the wounds
Of His troubled child?

Look through His eyes
At a suffering soul
What will you do?

We Knew Him

We knew Him long ago
Before we crossed the veil
Of forgetfulness

Our Father's firstborn Son
The Great I Am
Glorious Creator
Immortal Jehovah

Yet when He came to earth
Disguised as mortal man
His own knew him not
Despised Him
Rejected Him
Crucified Him

Would we have seen Him
For what He was?
Would we have known Him
In Bethlehem
In Nazareth
In Jerusalem
Or on the cross
As He died for us?

Trouble

Trouble will find us
It's what we're here for
Trials to bend
But not break us
To make our weak places
Strong in Him
To make us stretch
And reach
Until we grow
Tall enough
To reach up to Him
So He may reach down
And lift us up
Beside Him

The Things of My Soul

Like the prodigal
I wandered off
Into a far country
Seeking the things of the world
Leaving the things of my soul
Far behind
Ever shrinking
Growing small

At the edge of sight
They stayed with me
Keeping a safe distance
Whispering to my heart
Hoping I would look back
Through the mist
And see them
Shining there

Daily Prayer

I am Yours, Father
Do with me as You will
Turn my heart toward the poor
And the suffering

Send me to the weak in faith
That I may strengthen them
With Your words

Send me to the hungry
That I might share of my substance
Which You have given me

Send me to the lost
That I might help them
Find You

Send me to the sorrowful
That I may comfort them
With Your promise of joy

Send me to those who are angry
And those who are hurt
That I might calm their hearts
With Your peace

Do with me as You will, Father
For I am Yours, always and forever

This I pray in the sacred name
Of Your beloved Son, Jesus Christ
Who suffered and died that I might live
And have eternal joy in You
Amen

Faith & Doubt

Doubt is easy.
Just follow the path
Of least resistance
Into the world.
It runs downhill,
Coasting all the way
To the bottom.

Faith is the harder path.
Mortal eyes cannot see
Where it leads.
It is an uphill climb,
Step by stumbling step
Toward an invisible goal.

Whichever path you choose,
Ask yourself this question:
Where will I be
When I arrive?

ABOUT THE AUTHOR

Jane Starwood left the Church of Jesus Christ of Latter-day Saints at age 19 and returned at age 74, fully committed to serving her Heavenly Father, His Son Jesus Christ, and all who believe in them.

The poems in this volume grew out of Ms. Starwood's spiritual autobiography, *Memoirs of a Prodigal Daughter: Returning to the Church of Jesus of Latter-day Saints.*

Some of the poems in this
volume first appeared in

Memoirs of a Prodigal Daughter:
Returning to the Church
of Jesus Christ of Latter-day Saints

Read the full text at prodigalmemoirs.com.
Available soon in paperback and e-book.